Here Is the African Savanna

Madeleine Dunphy

ILLUSTRATED BY

Tom Leonard

Web of Life

CHILDREN'S BOOKS

Here is the African savanna.

H*ere is the grass*
that grows on the plain
which turns green or brown
depending on rain:
Here is the African savanna.

Here are the zebras
who eat the grass
that grows on the plain
which turns green or brown
depending on rain:
Here is the African savanna.

Here are the lions
who stalk the zebras
who eat the grass
that grows on the plain
which turns green or brown
depending on rain:
Here is the African savanna.

H*ere is the giraffe*
who watches the lions
who stalk the zebras
who eat the grass
that grows on the plain
which turns green or brown
depending on rain:
Here is the African savanna.

H
ere is the tree

which shades the giraffe

who watches the lions

who stalk the zebras

who eat the grass

that grows on the plain

which turns green or brown

depending on rain:

Here is the African savanna.

H*ere are the baboons*
who sit in the tree
which shades the giraffe
who watches the lions
who stalk the zebras
who eat the grass
that grows on the plain
which turns green or brown
depending on rain:
Here is the African savanna.

H*ere are the pods*
dropped by the baboons
who sit in the tree
which shades the giraffe
who watches the lions
who stalk the zebras
who eat the grass
that grows on the plain
which turns green or brown
depending on rain:
Here is the African savanna.

H*ere are the impalas*
who eat the pods
dropped by the baboons
who sit in the tree
which shades the giraffe
who watches the lions
who stalk the zebras
who eat the grass
that grows on the plain
which turns green or brown
depending on rain:
Here is the African savanna.

Here are the tick birds
who perch on the impalas
who eat the pods
dropped by the baboons
who sit in the tree
which shades the giraffe
who watches the lions
who stalk the zebras
who eat the grass
that grows on the plain
which turns green or brown
depending on rain:
Here is the African savanna.

H*ere are the hippos*

who are groomed by the tick birds

who perch on the impalas

who eat the pods

dropped by the baboons

who sit in the tree

which shades the giraffe

who watches the lions

who stalk the zebras

who eat the grass

that grows on the plain

which turns green or brown

depending on rain:

Here is the African savanna.

H
ere is the river

which is home to the hippos

who are groomed by the tick birds

who perch on the impalas

who eat the pods

dropped by the baboons

who sit in the tree

which shades the giraffe

who watches the lions

who stalk the zebras

who eat the grass

that grows on the plain

which turns green or brown

depending on rain:

Here is the African savanna.

Here is the elephant

who drinks from the river

which is home to the hippos

who are groomed by the tick birds

who perch on the impalas

who eat the pods

dropped by the baboons

who sit in the tree

which shades the giraffe

who watches the lions

who stalk the zebras

who eat the grass

that grows on the plain

which turns green or brown

depending on rain:

Here is the African savanna.

Here is the grass

that is food for the elephant

who drinks from the river

which is home to the hippos

who are groomed by the tick birds

who perch on the impalas

who eat the pods

dropped by the baboons

who sit in the tree

which shades the giraffe

who watches the lions

who stalk the zebras

who eat the grass

that grows on the plain

which turns green or brown

depending on rain:

Here is the African savanna.

Wildlife of the East African Savanna

YELLOW-BILLED OXPECKER
(Tick Bird)

ACACIA TREE

ACACIA PODS

AFRICAN
HIPPOPOTAMUS

BURCHELL'S ZEBRA

East Africa has an immense diversity of animal life. Nowhere else on earth can so many large animals be seen living together. Giraffes, elephants, lions, zebras, and hippos are just a few of the animals inhabiting the savanna.

Most of these animals are in some way dependent on grass for survival. Herbivores, such as the zebra, depend on grass directly for nourishment while carnivores, like the lion, hunt animals that subsist on grass. Without grass, neither could survive.

Just as the animals are dependent upon grass, the grass is dependent on rain. In East Africa, there are two seasons: the rainy season and the dry season. During the dry season, many animals, such as wildebeests, zebras, and gazelles, must go on long migrations in order to find enough grass to live. Carnivores sometimes follow these animals on their migrations.

OLIVE BABOON

MASAI LION

AFRICAN ELEPHANT

MASAI
GIRAFFE

IMPALA

Much of the wildlife of East Africa can be found within the boundaries of national parks in Tanzania and Kenya. Despite this protection, many animal populations have been greatly reduced and some are in danger of extinction. Even though these parks are animal sanctuaries, the rhinoceros and elephant are still being killed for their horns and tusks; leopards are being hunted for their fur; and herbivores are being killed for meat. Additionally, the limited areas of these parks and the recent ongoing drought have had negative impacts on these animals' populations.

We must act now to help ensure their survival. To find out what you can do, write to the African Wildlife Foundation, 1400 Sixteenth Street, N.W., Suite 120, Washington, D.C. 20036, or check out their website at www.awf.org.

For my beloved niece, Lucy.
—M.D.

For my sister, Magnus, my brothers, Chris, John, and Richard,
and my sister-in-law, Madeline.
—T.L.

Text ©1999 by Madeleine Dunphy.
Illustrations ©1999 by Tom Leonard.

First published in 1999 by Hyperion Books for Children.

For information, write to:
Web of Life Children's Books
P.O. Box 2726, Berkeley, California 94702

Published in the United States in 2006 by Web of Life Children's Books.

Printed in Singapore.

Cataloging-in-Publication Data is on file with the Library of Congress.

ISBN 0-9773795-2-3 (paperback edition)
978-0-9773795-2-1

ISBN 0-9773795-3-1 (hardcover edition)
978-0-9773795-3-8

The artwork for this book was prepared using acrylic.

Read all the books in the series:
*Here Is the Tropical Rain Forest, Here Is the Coral Reef, Here Is the Wetland,
Here Is the Southwestern Desert,* and *Here Is the Arctic Winter.*

For more information about our books, and the authors
and artists who create them, visit our website:
www.weboflifebooks.com

Distributed by Publishers Group West